antidote to her ruin.

POETRY

antidote to her ruin.

p.r.w.

atmosphere press

Published by Atmosphere Press

Cover design by Kevin Stone

Illustrations by Sara Feistel

Secondary illustrations by Kevin Stone

Editing by Matthew Vaughan

Secondary editing by Dr. Kyle McCord

Advisor: Dennis Mathew

atmospherepress.com

antidote to her ruin.

POETRY

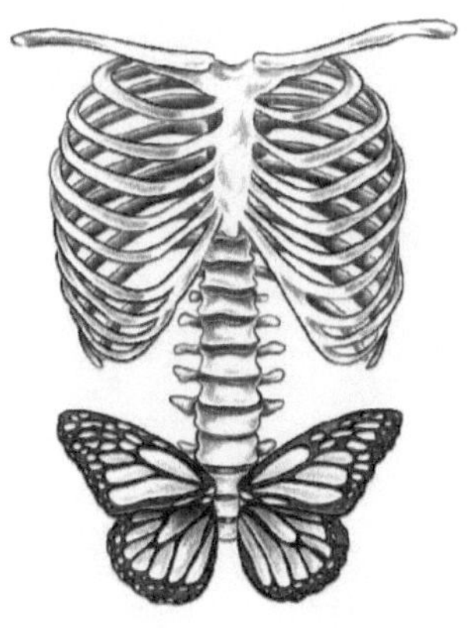

p.r.w.

and maybe that's the beauty of it all—
not the part where we find love,
but the part where we decide to try again when we've lost it.

table of contents

to all the ones i've ever loved—
and to one in particular.

—

to all the girls that
survived and overcame
heartbreak,
healing and found new growth
and beauty in the brokenness
deep within their bones.

to the girls that found themselves,
after him.

part one:
leaving.

her

When his love first found me,
I was bound by the wild pulsing throughout my bones.

I was never ready for his love
and the way it
shook me,
wrecked me—
in the most beautiful ways.

So I ran,
as far away from him as my weary lungs could suffice.
Until I found comfort in the restlessness,
in the lonely place I called my soul.

And once I loved him,
I lost him.

But his leaving seemed effortless.

her

My whole existence since knowing you
was running from you—
and

       eventually

          always

             coming back.

Coming and going
for five fucking years.

But you'd always let me back in,
and maybe it was because your soul
always recognized mine.
You'd let me in,
again and again—
and I think that's why I always come back to you.
Because coming back to you
feels like coming home.

You opened your arms
with each hello—
but then,
it was always just another
goodbye.

Your eyes begged me to stay,
but I chased a freedom that was slowly killing you inside.

And I never knew numb until now,
until instead of welcoming me inside your arms,
you welcome her.

After all,
I have only ever known leaving,
running
from every real thing I feel inside.
And I have finally realized my soul
was never meant to leave yours—
so now I'm running after you.
I remind myself that it might be too late.
So I pray,
beg,
plead
for yours to remember the familiar feeling,
the rush of holding me
after being gone for so long.
Instead of the ache of leaving—
feel the wild,
wild love
we will spend our whole lives trying to either tame
or run with.

And I remind myself,
that it might be

too late.

her

i
needed
his
love
most,
when
i
least
deserved
it.

internal warfare

I loved you with every ounce of my being.

But that's what restless hearts do—
we overthink,
we find every reason to not love you,
we doubt,
we question.
We find enough reason to stay,
enough reason to satisfy us just for a moment,
until the next breath of anxiety fill the lungs of our mind—
making reservations,
preparing its table,
claiming its seat.

And then,
when we've finally realized it *is* okay,
that there is no need to constantly pick apart
with our subconscious tendencies,
that it is the time to love
and to love fully,
to let our guard down
completely,
wholeheartedly
realizing that it was him all along—
who stayed,
who fought
for my attention when I was too broken

to be bothered by his unwavering
love,
kindness,
patience,
appreciation
for an often-halfhearted love
with a girl in constant battle with herself—
waging a civil war between
her head and her heart.

And once we've broken that barrier within us,
in knowing,
we wholeheartedly
love him,
want him,
need him
and then beg for him to stay—

    he leaves.

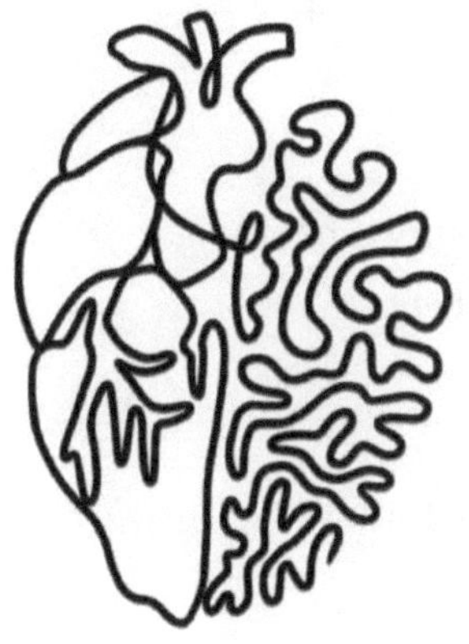

her

And if we're being honest—
he broke my heart.

I laid everything on the line
told him how I felt
gave him my heart . . .
something that took me
five years to do.
And he didn't even have the nerve
to hand it back to me,
to send it back
with the rest of all my other things.
He just left it all there
where it lay,
where it was—
and walked the fuck away.

Tell me how *that* doesn't teach a girl
to put chains around her heart?

her

And I'm so mad at you.
Why did you have to make me love you
and then leave?
I'm mad because you made me love you,
and then
you did what I have always done—
leave.

And still,
you left.

her

And maybe all along,
God was teaching me how to be alone—
because He knew
that was one day

something I would be.

her

And when the light fades to black,
I'll still be reaching for you in a quiet room:
four walls surrounding,
enclosing emptiness—
cold sheets
and the constant ache
of missing you with me.

And when darkness becomes day,
I'll wake to the sun
and a breeze through my curtains
with the smell of rain—
leaving goosebumps across the skin
you used to kiss with your fingertips.

I'll lay awake,
in the bed I made
tangled in the madness I try to tame—
fractured heartbeats
rattling within the walls of my rib cage.

And I can't breathe.
I forgot how.

Every inhale,
every exhale—
there is only the ache of
your leaving.

> *And it's leaving scars.*

her

Missing you has become of me.
It is not
when that I am missing you—
it is that I am *always* missing you.
And missing you
never leaves.
There is no in-between
in which I miss you,
and I do not.

—

today
was
just
another
day
of
missing
you.

her

One day I am going to wake up
and feel nothing for you.
Nothing when I see a picture of you with her,
nothing when I see you walk in the door
of the same bar we used to go to.
I'm going to feel nothing when a memory floods my mind,
when I catch your eye from across the room—
when I finally don't have to convince myself
of all the pretty lies
in pretending that you were never mine.
I'm going to feel nothing when I wake up from a dream
with you in it,
nothing when I hang out with our old friends
and they mention your name.
There will be no familiarity to it—
just another name.

One day I'm going to feel nothing,
but I feel everything today.

her

i
lost
myself
in a
million little moments
with you.

     and i'm just trying to find my way back.

her

His skin and my skin wrote poetry.
Black ink and feather quills drawing an escape,
fragments of reality and make-believe
bleeding into existence,
seeping into the other—
something magical,
something more than what we could have ever become
on our own.
But nonetheless a story.

And now we are only forgotten poetry—
from a book that seems to have never been written,
never to rest on his bookshelf . . .
on his empty,
dusty bookshelf.

And I cannot breathe,
with the thought of never loving another one,
another him.

her

And I want to write of you
until my pen finds the last edge.
The last drop of ink.
The last lonely reader—

even if it's just me.

And if one day
we are defined by the things that we loved—
I hope to have been written in you,
defined by you.

her

but

trying

to

find

the

words

to

describe

loving

you

is

like

trying

to

map

a

lost

city—

in ruins and pointless.

her

And I'm mad at her,
jealous even.
Mad at the way she touches your skin,
full palms in places only my fingertips have been.
Jealous of the way your eyes beg to meet hers,
the way they used to with mine,
before.

—

maybe
he's
just
trying
to
make
sense
of
it
all,
in
another's
arms.

her

You can take as much time as you need—
but when you're done trying to convince yourself she's me,
you'll be watching us both leave.

her

Damnit.
I want to hate you—
you've given me a hundred reasons to.
But the real reason I want to hate you is because

I still love you.

And he only remembers loving me.

her

The hardest part
of it all
was to have gone from deeply loving you,
to forever missing you.

But having bittersweet withdrawals
with every
s
   t
     e
       p
along the way—
because at least it came with a memory
of your face.

unsettled souls

I've just been thinking about you lately . . .
wondering how you've been.
And I can't decide if I love that
or
hate it—
but I think it's somewhere in between.

her

I've never been more lost than I have been in losing you.
But you found her,
and I am slowly making my way back to me—
and maybe that's okay.
I guess
there are just some things you
fall from,
and fall to.

Sometimes the falling is all that's left.

her

I keep reminding myself that I have to forget you,
to erase you from my mind.
To let you slip from my memory
like my childhood phone number
or the Pythagorean theorem—
like all the things that were once ingrained in me.
To find memories without you in them,
even though I know I never will.

And I wake up with every intention to forget you,
but I know they are only lies.

her

time
only
p a s s e s
and
i
still
love
you.

—

There will always be the me that still loves you—
that person will never cease to exist,
as long as my heart is beating
inside my chest.

antidote to her ruin.

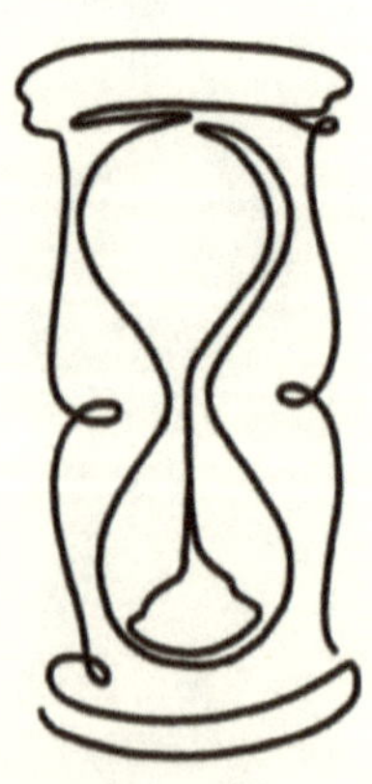

her

I don't know how to go back
to being strangers with someone
who has seen my soul.

her

And I still have dreams of him.
Vivid dreams.
But those around me tell me they are just that—

dreams.

I dream of him in the way he used to kiss me on rooftops.
The way his cold hands used to reach for me
under warm sweaters and firelight,
the woodlands,
lit up by a million little stars and fireflies.
I dream of him in car rides home,
winding down backroads,
my fingers tracing the little rivers of rain droplets running,
the FM static of the radio humming between us
and the flooding feeling of falling in love;
but I never told him
and he told me a hundred times before
that he did.
I dream of him in shades of blue and black,
in the bruises on my heart,
left from what is now considered our past—
and I don't want it to be.
The haunting of his ghost surrounds me and tortures me
in the way things used to be,
in the way he used to brush away the hair with his fingertips
when it fell in my face,

and kiss me that much more often when I wore red lipstick,
or when he read poetry and the words melted like autumn
into winter with the snow.
The way he promised forever with a diamond ring
he bought for me,
but decided to give to her.

But I guess it's better than not having him at all.

her

I didn't mean to break my own heart when I let him go.

But I never really realized before,
that love was worth risking *everything* for.
I had risked it all,
and still lost.
But the truth is,
given the chance—
I'd risk it all,
all over again
for a love as mad as ours.

her

Perhaps he was the love of my life—
and if he was not,
he was the only one worth breaking my own heart for.

But how do you know?
How does anyone ever *really* know?

her

It's been said that we all have to lose a love in our life,
so we recognize it once it finally comes back around—
again.

And that feels like bullshit.

part two:
if he loved her.

him

What is it about *me* that you've never been able to get over,
never been able to find in someone else,
no matter how hard you tried?
What made you keep coming back?
What made you miss *me*?
What do you think about when we're not together,
or even not speaking?
What are the parts of *me* that creep in,
in your dreams?

her

Why *me*?!
What makes *me* so damn special
of all the girls
you've ever fallen for,
ever loved?
What is it about *me*?
Why did you want *me*,
love *me*?
Why did *your* heart
always wait on *me*?

And why, when I ran *for you*
with my guard down completely,
and my heart
w i d e   o p e n,
did *you* leave?

–

I finally figured it out, didn't I—
why you ran when I told you I loved you?
It's because you loved the me that didn't want you,
that ran from you—
and you didn't know it until I finally said I loved you,
too.

The me you didn't have to chase.

After five years of waiting for me
and still,
without even a fight or the mention of my name—
you decided to leave.

> Or maybe you couldn't fathom loving me and
> losing me,
> *again.*

her

And the last time we spoke,
you were distant
and I was hurting—
from all the words you refused to say.

calling out for you

How to teach a heart patience,
when it knows exactly what it's wanted
all along?

You.

—

I think I'll always wonder about you.

lovesick and wounded

you

can

give

your

whole

heart

and

it

can

still

not

be

enough.

—

What a cruel,
mysterious world—
that even love *sometimes*
is
not
enough.

her

Why does my heart beg to leave my chest?
How do you quiet a restless heart?

How do you tame the wild pulse
held within the cages of my skin?
How do you tame a wild beast
when it begs to escape?
When all along its only known confinement,
a prisoner of the mind.

Once it knew what it felt like to finally be loved by yours,
I knew it would never be the same.

44

her

I know I'm supposed to slowly forget you,
but I can't stop loving you.
And I secretly hope you're going through the same thing:
missing me,
wanting me
in every way.

I hope you miss the way your fingertips felt on my skin,
running down my back,
your hands in my hair,
your chest on mine.
I hope you miss slow dancing on hardwood floors
and telling me you love me
and asking if it's okay if you say it out loud.
And I smile
and kiss you
because I feel the same way,
but I'm too afraid to tell you after five years.
I hope when you drive through the city,
you have to do everything in your power
to keep from turning
down my street.
I hope when you hear that song,
you think of the night I told you
Zach Bryan had written it just for us,
and you lose your breath—
because I'm not next to you

holding your hand while you listen,
and the lyrics hit you
because they're wrapped in me.
I hope when your head hits the pillow
you remember mine laying next to yours,
and you have to roll over
away from the other side of the bed
because you can't stand the cold,
empty sheets—
where you used to reach for me.
Or maybe,
you reach for her.

I hope when your mom asks how you've been
you stumble on your words
because you can't get past the catch in your throat.
I hope you miss me when it storms—
I hope you damn the rain
and it reminds you I'm gone.
I hope when you wrap your hand around a bottle,
you close your eyes
and press it against your lips,
it takes you back to my 22nd birthday
at a bonfire
in the middle of nowhere,
under the stars.
Me, dancing around in the firelight
with ash in my hair,
drinking wine out of the bottle and

smiling at you.
I hope when you hit a back road
you think about the night you kissed me for the first time,
and the time after that
when I climbed over into your lap.
I hope you miss me and remember me
in the flashing lights of an arcade,
laughing at you in a room full of people—
two kids discovering what it means to feel free
in the presence of another.

I hope you decide you miss me.

him

She looks like you in the reflection of my window,
lining her lips with lipstick in the rearview and
laughing through her teeth.
And maybe her hands feel like your hands
walking through the street:
flashing lights and stop signs and crosswalks
where we used to jaywalk
to tiny coffee shops and
you would find the farthest corner booth and
I would order whatever you ordered
because I could never pronounce the names right.
But I'd always add whipped cream to mine
because I loved the way you looked at me
when it tickled my nose.
So now I order for her
and hold the whipped cream.

But when it rains,
I think of you.
Because she runs for cover
or pulls out an umbrella,
instead of standing in the middle of it to feel it—
she's not like you in that way.

hopeless recovery

How do you mend the pieces of your own heart—
when someone else has it in the palm of their hands?

49

—

the
endless
misery
in
waiting
for
repair.

her

And I want my bones to be buried next to your bones,
six feet under dead flowers and stone.
To be at peace with the way I loved you in this world—
and if not in this lifetime,
then maybe in the afterlife.

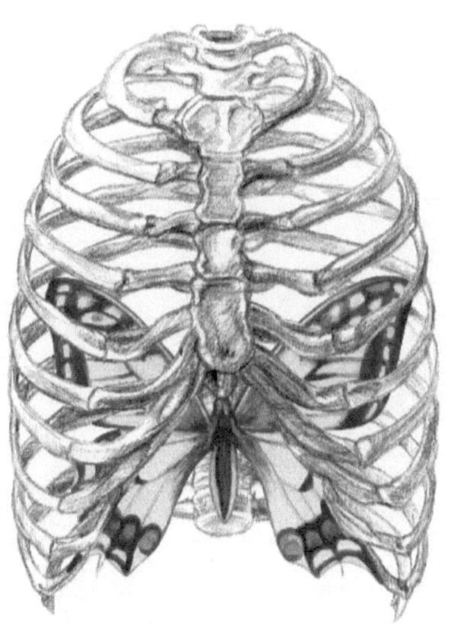

her

if
he
loved
me,
he
would.

her

How to tell a heart that it's supposed to move on,
get over him?
The mind often listens,
but never the heart.

It chooses to stay—
in the thought,
in the motion,
in the very moment of endless ruin,
in still loving him,
again and again and again and again.

How to tell a heart,
convince a heart that he is no longer worth loving?

her

Everything I am trying to hold on to has already parted,
already walked away—
and it's time I do the same.
I'll put one foot in front of the other now,
even if I have to drag myself.

her

It's a waste of time,
a waste of breath
to hold on to someone who is no longer worth loving.
Because in life and everything else
while you're suspended in thin air,
in all its nothingness—
besides the exception of existence,
there is just that,
nothingness:
where tears refuse to fall,
defying gravity,
in broken hearts that have fallen and
beat for a man that hasn't given even a thought more
for you.
It is slowly sucking the life out of you,
sis.

And you don't deserve drowning in his CO_2.

her

And you'll keep running.

And I'll keep building every wall I ever put up
a little

t
a
l
l
e
r.

her

Someday—
I'm going to find
an old photograph of us,
and that familiar tinge of pain will remind me
again,

        that we no longer exist.

her

And maybe so in remembering you—
years from now,
when the wounds of my heart have long scarred together,
the dull ache will remind me

to remember you.

her

I am trying to forget you.
But I find that awfully and terribly beautiful.
        Even still.

Because I will keep trying to forget you,
slowly,
and you will have already forgotten me.
But in time,
you will try to remember me
and every part of me slipping from you,
falling farther from what touched you so deeply before,
wondering helplessly where we would be if maybe
we'd have stayed.

And I will no longer wish for butterflies in my heart,
flying out the top of my skull when I hear your name.
The skin on my shoulders will cringe,
feeling an unfamiliar touch from another
but I won't wish for yours.
I will no longer dance at the foot of my bed
in my underwear and your holy sweater
when our song comes on and
my hairbrush will only stay meant for brushing hair.
I will no longer feel the warmth of your breath
on my cold nose
in the middle of December,
chattering teeth whispering, "hold me closer,"

and your hands fit around mine,
enclosing ten fingers and palmfuls of maybe,
forevers.
Or when I kissed you at red lights and
our whole world slowed the flow of traffic and
angered tempers and impatient,
quick-triggered fingers,
honking horns from rattling automobiles;
but your eyes—
deafening the world around us,
while everything else stood still.
I will just stand still—
with rose-colored glasses at my feet.

Because I won't remember,
and you will.

Because now I paint over gold,
vintage picture frames of us,
hanging on walls with fragile beams and cracks in the ceiling,
falling debris and dust from the seams.
I will remember it then.
When black covers white picket fences and
rust-colored flowers,
emerald shades of velvet curtains and drapings and
rain dripping through old window panes,
broken blinds letting dimming,
shyly-faded light in,
and there's a piano in the corner,

dressed in ivory,
longing to fill the room again
with rich tones demanding its attention,
tall, elongated candlesticks
with molds of dripping wax from ash-colored wicks,
and expensive chandeliers filled with cobwebs and moths
reminding me my heart no longer lives here
in this vacancy—
in the memories we used to keep.
Empty suitcases stacked
with handwritten love letters discarded around them,
"to her, to him,"
where a lost love language was abandoned
and where it doesn't exist.
Like broken mirrors scattered around bare feet,
filled with disappointment and redundantly painful steps
over dirty concrete neglected to be swept and
white sheets covering the remains of who we used to be
and breathe.
Even I know we were rare.
A beautiful tragedy—
the mess of you and me.

And suddenly,
like the leaves—
I, too, fell and left.
But honey,
it's not always as it seems.

her

I used to paint you in shades of gold,
but now

I'll paint for me.

a love affair disarmed

The scarring of what remains:
raw and exposed,
gunpowder and smoke covering our shoelaces;
an innocent wildfire gone up in flames,
igniting and exploding,
burned to the flat surface of the earth,
saturated in soot,
exhaling from the cracks of where everything is broken—
what's left of a no longer existing love,
the tempted forgotten remains.
A fallen beautiful mess in warfare.
Disarmed.

In the ruin of you and I.

her

and
still,
my
skin
was
left
in
scars
of
all
the
places
you
used
to
kiss
me.

her

You're the kind of love I will tell my children about—
it's a shame they won't have your eyes.

her

I found God in the darkest depths of losing you.

When I cried out for your love,
I found God.
When I wished for your presence,
I found God.
When I prayed for your breath in my lungs,
your heart against my chest,
I found God.

I cried on the bathroom floor for hours,
often nights.
I cried until my eyes were swollen and my bones were tired.
I cried when there was nothing more left to exhale.
Until I was numb to the feeling of life
pulsing through my veins,
numb to the feeling of pain.
Until lying on the bathroom floor,
alone and in need of a Savior—
I found God.

In losing you, I surrendered.

her

You have been hanging onto my heart
like tumbleweed,
wrapped in barbed wire—
tugging,
pulling,
ripping
until it bleeds.

I cut the wire,
untied your tangle
and watched you fall
as I finally fell for me.

I watched my wings take me
far,
far
away
from you—
as I left you,
bleeding from all the places you once hurt me.

her

i
found
my
wings
when
i
fell.

–

And maybe sometimes
all it takes to find your wings,
is the fall.

her

It is okay to fall out of love,
to leave a love that no longer stirs the wings of butterflies
in a heart.

It is okay to walk away in shoes that haven't yet been dirtied
from the earth's raw filth,
scarring the surface
of all the beautiful places you haven't before been.

It is okay to be alone,
to choose yourself for a damn moment in time.

It is okay to find freedom in the wings he gave you
when he let you go and left you to fall.

And eventually,
it will be okay to stay for someone.
But for now,
while you're holding your own hand and
mending your broken pieces,
it's okay to stop loving another.
To instead
relearn how to love yourself.

her

Loving him was never the sole earth-shattering moment
like they oftentimes claim it to be:
the earth seemingly revolving around who you love and
how they love you is not when or where it happens;
but the magic that comes with finding yourself after them,
when you didn't have them telling you who you are,
and finally finding out for yourself and loving you
after all this time—
that's the moment.

That's where the magic happens.

her

Patience,
I used to despise you.
I used to fear you.
I used to cringe with anxiety
and a sudden aching pain at the thought of you.
Until I had to find you,
until I had no choice but to learn you,
know you,
use you.
I realized there was faith in you,
hope even.
I learned
faith,
hope
and your name
nearly go hand in hand—
and that there is healing in you
and beauty,
all the same.
I found peace within you.
I found growth.
I found myself—
entangled in you
and there is nothing more rewarding
or confirming than that.
I found grace wrapped in you.

I found everything I was looking for,
really.
I found it all in the waiting,
in you—
patience.

her

When I was uncomfortable,
when I was hurting.
When my lungs begged to exhale a scream.
When my knees shook,
collapsed in the thought of moving forward.
When my heart cried for all the things it once held
that no longer existed in its presence.
When my hands felt the hard,
cold floors beneath them
and found a familiarity in feeling hard,
cold floors beneath them.
When my eyes saw only past time—
memories,
motions
of what they once saw and tended to cling to.
When my eyes refused to see again,
when my eyes only knew of *you*.
When my lips only remembered the touch of yours,
your breath and the 'I love you's
interrupted intentionally
by mine.
I found patience in
losing and waiting
for you.
I found patience
in the constant ache of looking for you,
remembering you.

I found patience in the darkest moment of my life.

In losing and waiting for you,
I found myself—

without you.

her

And of all the things I thought I would never recover from—
I still

survived you.

her

I don't dream about him like I used to,
like I want to.
Those vivid dreams that used to invade my sleep—
they are kinder now,
more respectful,
more understanding that I need
s p a c e.

I wish they knew that I missed them—

dreams.

him

she
will
never
be

you.

her

Maybe the hardest things to let go of
were never really ours to begin with.

Maybe that is, in fact,
why they are so hard to let go.

her

He reached in and pulled the life right out of me.
A suffocation I would have died all over again for,
      and also lived.

But I found myself in the depths of his absence,
in a heartbreak that was slowly killing me,
but still breathing life into these aching lungs and bones.

I learned how I heal.
I learned the way I see the world without him in it.
I learned how I live within the simplicity and complexity
of existence,
and the agony left in embers from the devastation of ruin
his leaving left.
And how it is so clearly,
vividly—
poetry.
And so I started to live my life in verse.

I learned distraction is humanity's first thought in healing
and that there is no true healing in distraction—
only that of distraction itself.

I learned healing is much messier than we often let on,
and that everything about the world of grief and all its antics
is mostly gray.
There is no sure, certain way through any of it.

So, I took the time to get to know myself again.
To ground myself instead of tiptoeing around through the
bitterness,
the anger,
the sadness
held within the grips of letting go.

To plant my bare feet on the earth
so that I could feel everything,
and to feel it deeply.

All of it:
the hurt
the pain
the resentment
the fear.
           To see what the pain had to offer me.

And then to leave it there and move on,
like you eventually did
from me.

her

I have come to the realization
and acceptance in that I will never truly be over the situation,
over him—
but maybe I have moved on.
There is an obvious difference between the two.
And that is okay.

Progress is a process
and healing will forever be messy.
Even still,
in the pursuit of happiness after heartbreak.

part three:
yet to be tamed.

her

And you showed up at my doorstep,
with your head hanging towards your feet—
you looked at me with blue eyes
that begged to be seen,
shrugged your shoulders and said,
"I'm sorry for leaving,
I still love you—
do you still love me?"

My eyes wandered around the words
slipping from your mouth,
my head and my heart
colliding,
fighting;
but—
I looked at you
and I told you without even saying,
without a sound.

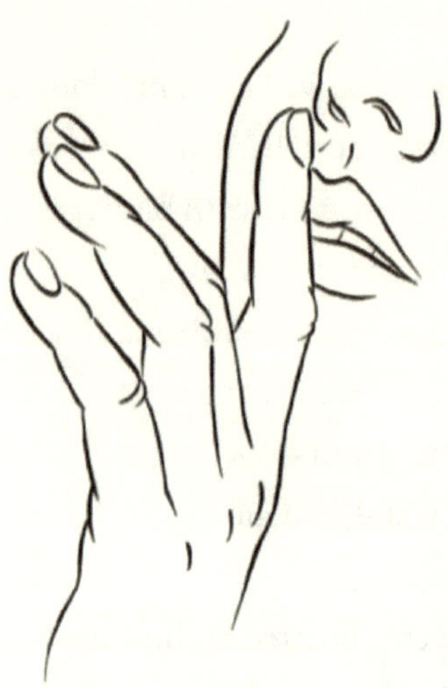

her

I told him I loved him with my eyes—
but the mouth that wanted to kiss him,
told him to leave.

And he did.

—what I have always done.

her

and
i
chased
away
the
butterflies
as
he
left.

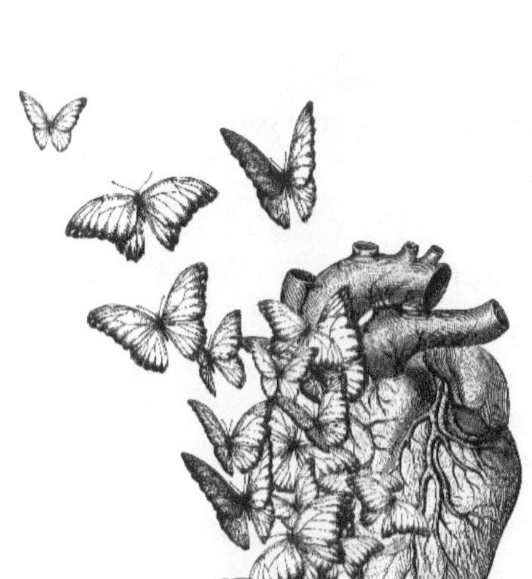

her

If I had it my way,
I'd kiss your neck,
your face,
and touch my fingertips
along your waist,
take your t-shirt off
and then,
kiss your chest.

I'd want to be way too close to you,
for you,
with you;
too close for you to forget—
to say goodbye.

all's fair in love and war

Sometimes loving can be painful,
yet all the while painfully beautiful.
Sometimes it takes great bravery to love recklessly,
fearless of the great fall
and then the always inevitable collapse,
without hesitation in the wounding of its wars,
the ruin it sometimes leaves,
because the battle will have been worth it.
But if at first it weren't for great bravery,
there would be no great love.

Not all love is meant to last forever,
but it doesn't mean that it wasn't exceptional,
even if only for a moment.

her

I told Emily about you today.

"He not only loved me for me,
but for all that I was,
for all that I was not,
all that I have been
and strive to be—
good and bad,
bad and ugly;
but he loved me in all the ways that I just simply existed.

And God,
I love him."

her

Loving him
left me in ruin—
but I would have gone to war a million times
to have felt his love

even once.

the wreckage

Sometimes I need to be wrecked to feel again.

her

Maybe,
in the mess of it all,
I will find you.
I will find you and me together,
still,
dancing in the chaos of the rain,
when a hundred people are running for cover around us,
and we are wildly existing with one another—
under
what falls for us,
chasing us with lightning bolts and thundering aches
of what it feels like to be a storm—
what it feels like to be alive,

    to be so fearlessly alive.

her

Isn't it beautiful that you and I,
we got to

exist

in the same lifetime—
together?

her

You and I,
finding beauty in the brokenness.

him

'cause
honey
this
ain't
over—

it
ain't
over
baby.

her

And he came back,
crashing through the door,
tears running down his face to the lips that kissed me.
He grabbed me,
sat me on the countertop by the sink
and told me he loved me—
that he's always loved me,
and that he wanted me
more than anything else in his entire existence.
And I loved him,
too—
more than I've ever loved anything or anyone,
with every part of my soul.

   But . . .

her

Maybe distance is the only way we know how
to love each other.
Because I think we both know if we loved fully,
we wouldn't survive its destruction—
it would be the end of us both.

And I think we both know
that we could never
lose or love
the other again,
without completely being consumed.
Left without any oxygen in our lungs,
starved of the air that used to breathe down our spines,
taming what's held within the cages of our ribs—
all the while driving it mad,
wild.

And yet,
if we were to give it a name,
we wouldn't know what to call it or
where to even begin.

her

Because I still exist within the subtle tragedies of his ruin.
He begs of me to relive them,
so that he doesn't have to forget them,
forget me.

And maybe that is the beauty of never really moving on,
because I once lived within his,
and he still chooses to.

To try—
existing within the ruins of one another.

seeds of reconciliation

And the words falling from your lips,
latching on to every fiber in my bones
reminds me that even in the state of pain,
there is love—
and that they
can somehow still coexist.

And maybe, so can we.

part four:
the feeling of falling and fighting.

her

We were running back roads past midnight,
teasing you with the idea of playing
critter, critter.

And you told me you were holding out on kissing me
until maybe the second date—
because I looked like one of those girls that are always kissed
on the first.

And still,
I asked, "Why?"

You looked at me,
slammed on your brakes,
and you grabbed my face as you kissed me.
And it was the best,
most unforeseen,
hearts crashing moment I have ever had.

And still to this day—
that was the best first kiss I have had.
Maybe the best kiss I have *ever* had.
You took the breath out of my lungs with that kiss—
and I'm still searching for that lack of oxygen.

 Even now.

him

Your music was playing loud
and you were screaming lyrics at the top of your lungs,
bare feet on the ground,
feeling the naked earth beneath you.
And you were spinning around,
making me come undone,
unraveling me a little more with every turn.
Your silhouette in the fire,
wild with the flame,
all with a bottle hanging from your hand.

And you were dancing.
I don't know what's wilder.

Your gentle lips
dressed in wine,
if they begged of me to kiss them,
how could I have said no?
Oh, if I could only have held your hand—
but your soul,
I could not tame.
　　　　But would I want to?

—

And I loved you even then,
untamed.

109

her

And it was never cigarettes or liquor,
nicotine or alcohol
to get me addicted,
to make me drunk.
Cocaine or weed;
it wasn't adenosine
or any other type of drug
that made my heart stop.

No, that was you.

him

She was everything all at once—
that girl.
She was brilliant
and wonderful
and magnificent
and fearless.
And wild,

man—

she was *w i l d.*

I miss her.

what the wildflowers taught me

You picked a flower just for me,
beside the dirt road,
along the creek—
a wildflower.
You held my hand and I held yours.
The summer breeze
whispers, "to roam."
Petals to the wind,
begging to be loved,
"He loves me,
he loves me not."

His hand in her hand,
a wildflower in the other—
one last petal to leave . . .

He loves her.

him

You never told me you loved me,
but I have always known.

no
one
looks
at
just
anyone

    like that.

her

What makes me think I need you?

Maybe it's the way your soul calls for mine
or maybe it's the gravel in your voice,
the way your eyes cut through.

The way you like the gold in my hair
and how my tiny hands fit inside
the creases in the calluses of yours.

> Maybe it's the way everything about *you*
> and *yours*,
> fits perfectly with *me*
> and *mine*.

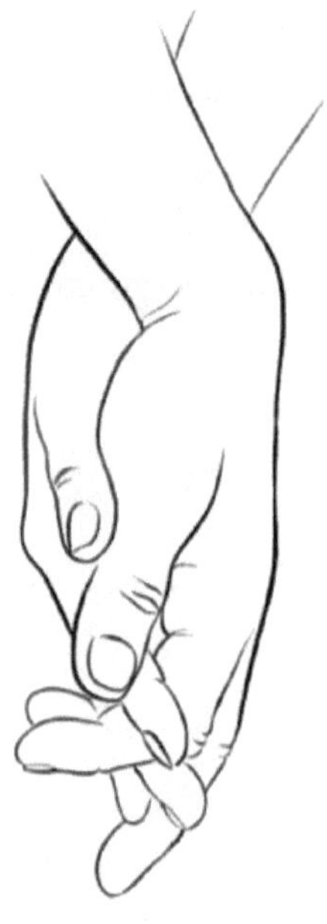

her

"Tell me," she said,
"what is true love supposed to look like, anyway?"

And he started searching the crowd,
as if he were looking for the answer
in a city of strangers.

him

"Well, I'm not sure. But I would imagine it looks
a lot like home and a little bit wild,"
and then he looked at her,
"I would imagine."

moment of impact

my
love
for
you
was
always
within
the
collision
of
where
you
began,
and
where
i
ran.
until
you
left.

—

the
collision
and
descent
of

you and i.

her

And he was the most real thing I have ever touched.
I haven't felt anything close

> to what I did within the warmth of his hands—
> wrapped in mine,
> wrapped around me.

I wish I didn't always feel like leaving,
I wish I would have stayed.

even
all
those
years
ago . . .

him

cast
these
stones,
play
with
my
heartstrings,
tear
at
my
bones.

—

I would suffer a million times over—
if it meant holding you just for a moment
more.

him

"Are you scared of me?"

her

"I'm not scared of you,
just scared to love you."

Because I know who I would be without you.
I've met her.

her

scared
to
love

–

scared
to
leave.

defense mechanisms

How dare I run from the things I feel the most—
from what makes me feel alive
and in love
and too much?

Why do I run
from the things
I would bleed for?

her

You changed *everything.*

Everything I thought was love,
everything I thought to be love,
what I thought it was supposed to be—
or anything close to it.
It was all a lie until I met you,
until I loved you.

In you,
I learned how to not only love myself
in the exact moments that I exist,
but to let someone love me within the moments
that I am living them;
in the exception of just that—
existing
in every version of me.

You taught me to embrace every season I go through,
every version of myself that I mold from and into,
and that it is okay to not always be okay.
That the right one will hold you through it,
asking nothing of you
other than for you to just let them hold you.

You taught me what a fearless kind of love feels like—
with no thought from this moment
to the next.

To just feel my way through it
and to lead with my heart,
instead.

You taught me that our eyes have just as many conversations
as our mouths do—
and that they are my favorite way of speaking,
my favorite language.

You taught me that the right person will know
exactly how you feel,
what you're thinking
before you even have to speak,
sometimes before *you* even know how you
feel
or think.
And that one single look,
motion
can give you away to the man that knows you
like the back of his hand—
the man who took the time to learn you.

You taught me that as hard as I try
I cannot hide from someone who knows every depth
to my soul.

You taught me what a selfless,
unconditional love means
and what it looks like.
And that mine
looks like you.

her

i
cannot
consciously
pretend
that
i
don't
love
you
anymore.

her

I've never been good at holding onto my words—
but neither have you.

So hold my hand
and look into my eyes,
while I say too much.

—

so
we
can
either
love
or
leave
and
let
go.

her

Do you remember all those years ago,
when you told me that you would wait for me?
And I told you not to.
To move on
because I didn't know what I wanted at the time.
But you stayed when I asked you to leave
and left when I asked you to stay.
But your heart never left mine.

And still,
your heart waited.
Even if we lost our way for a little while.
You eventually found your way back to me,
we both did.

But I'm really,
       really glad you did.

him

I will wait for you,
until the last breath in my lungs leave,
and I'll be on my way to loving you even then—
in the next life.

I will love you all the while I can,
in all the perfect moments you allow me to.
I will love you,

u n t i l

her

I remember the exact moment
I knew I was in love with you—
after five years,
five long fucking years
of slowly,
falling in love with you.
It was February—
we were slow dancing in the spare bedroom
of my best friend's house,
and we didn't even know we were dancing.
We were just standing there—
my head against yours,
my arms wrapped around your neck,
your hands wrapped around my waist
pulling me in.
We were just swaying back and forth with our eyes closed,
at 4 a.m. and there was no music playing—
just us,
in silence
with the wood floors groaning beneath us.
You looked at me,
and you told me you loved me.
And I wasn't afraid of loving you.

That was it—
the moment I knew.

Five years of pretending I didn't love you,
and all it took was that moment
to know,
I have loved you all this time.
I couldn't *not* feel what I feel for you anymore.
In that moment—
and all the other moments,
I knew.

Then,
and so many other times,
you felt so much like home
and everything wild
I had ever wanted to feel with a person—
I felt them all with you.

But no one ever taught me how to stay.

her

What your eyes did to my soul,
is something I cannot write down on this paper
with the pen my heart bleeds from.

–

Deeper than I've ever gone,
farther than I've ever fallen.
And so,
I ran—
terrified of the destruction you would bring me.

What your eyes did to my soul,
I knew with every part of me they'd be what destroyed me—
in the best and worst possible ways.
So I would always leave before they had the chance to.

her

"You don't fall in love with a body,
you fall in love with a soul.
And once in love with a soul,
everything about that body
becomes beautiful."

So I fell in love with you and yours,
slowly
for five years—
and then suddenly,
all at once.
And now I can't unsee
or unfeel
this beauty
standing before me.

In the wake of furiously loving you.

her

and
i
loved
you.
even
still,
in
all
our
ruin—
i
love
you.

her

and
i
cannot
help
my
heart.

—

I cannot help my heart in the way that it loves you,
in the way that it just assumes it needs yours
to be able to function—

to beat within the lonely skeleton it calls home.

But it does.

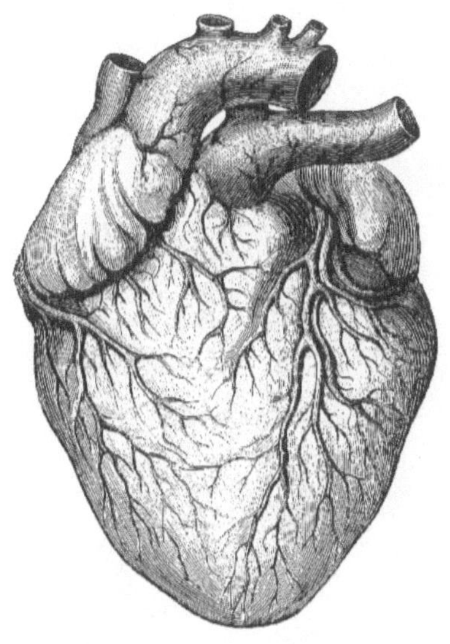

her

And in between the moments of fiercely loving you,
in all the beautiful chaos—
I found an undeniable strength
and beauty in pain and brokenness,
between the breaths of existing without you,
and that I can exist without you,
but that I don't want to.

poison vs. antidote

I'd rather risk it all with you than settle for a
simple, ordinary
love.
I'd rather have all of your wild
than wonder the rest of my life
if loving you is worth it.
Wonder if it could be—
with us.
If loving you was everything
I've searched for in every other love.
If loving you was the reason
for the breath inside of my lungs.
. . . *I'd rather*.

> I'd rather love you for a while,
> than to have never loved you at all.

we've been here before

Even if loving you meets pain—
I will still love you then.

> *—in the messiness of a heart breaking*
> *in the palm of another's hands.*

and

we wear the scars.

her

And I told him
if he ever had the notion to kiss me,
to kiss me with purpose—
to *really* kiss me.

    So he did.

        A kiss that didn't leave me starving of oxygen,
        but a kiss to fill my lungs.

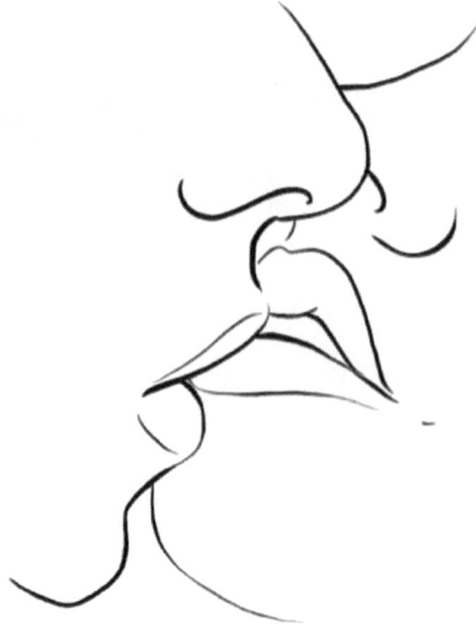

part five:
to stay.

him

These calluses line my fingertips,
from these guitar strings my soul longs to pick,
leaving creases in-between the skin that touches you.
Thunder rattling through my bones,
escaping my lungs in raspy melody;
and you're sitting beside me on the couch,
listening and looking at me—
something I never thought I would
see,
touch,
hold,
feel,
breathe

     again.

her

I lie on the couch
dressed in black lingerie—
watching you pick guitar,
watching your eyes fall to mine,
listening to you sing
as I run my fingers through your hair.

—

and
the
flood
of
my
sin
pours
over
me—
with
every
touch
of
your
skin.

in your atmosphere

I'd rather watch your eyes searching my body,
watch your lips beg to kiss mine,
watch your hands discover places
they've never before been—
than watch the thunder and rain
crash around us.

I'd rather *feel* it instead.

her

i
was
tired
of
loving
him
quietly.
tonight,
i
decided
to
love
him
out
loud.

her

And we were drunk,
together—
wrapped in the covers,
wrapped in each other
kissing and searching
for each other
in the dark.

My new favorite memory with you,
was watching you love all of me,
with all of you.

him

And what a time we had,
laughing in the mess of the sheets,
praying to God that this—
whatever it was,
would never end.

her

And now that I've gotten a taste of you—
I cannot get you off my tongue.
I cannot stomach the thought of you speaking mouthfuls
of useless words slipping from the lips
that whisper into my ear.
And there is a bitterness.

I want you to want me, too.
I want you to ache in the missing of me.
Like I have for you.

I want you to want me, need me.
I want you to breathe me in
until the lungs held within the cages of your ribs
feel as if they were suffocating
in the raw scent of my skin
against yours;
in the wild of night,
growing even wilder in love—
with only my clammy body
melting into yours.

I want you to feel me,
to be absolutely and
completely immersed in me.
Captivated by me.

I want your eyes,
mesmerized by my silhouette dancing in the mirror.

But mostly,
I want more than just moments with you.
I want to wake beside you
knowing
that this is forever.

And then,
I can rest my head next to your shoulder,
watching your eyelashes dream of all our
somedays and tomorrows.

him

You take my breath away in moments I least expect—
even all my thoughts.

You decide to fill every space
within the pockets of my mind,
during those last few breaths between sleep and wake.

And I am surrounded by you,
bound by the perfect imperfections you call your flaws.
I am captivated by you.
And in *this* moment,
I cannot wrap my mind around the fact that
I get to love you.

in the state of my existence

you

are

my

wildest

dream.

her

This morning with you
is as close to eternity as it gets—
when I look in your eyes,
yours draw right back into mine
and your skin is against my skin,
listening to the rain come down
as it begins to fall again.
And it's just us together,
in the simplicity of you
and you holding me;
existing next to the other—
your lips
and every whisper,
deep laughter,
sloppy kisses
and every word spilling from your mouth
like the coffee staining the cover of the book
laying next to me.
And I smile,
knowing
wholeheartedly
that I could spend all my
Sundays
with you.

coming to my senses

His eyes.
His hands.
His crooked smile.
His soul.
His voice.

But God,
his eyes,
his hands,
his crooked smile,
his soul,
his voice

—and all the ways they touched me.

her

Something about him that makes me want to go to church—
to worship the gods that made him.

her

And I sit naked in the tub
as you read poetry
and sit in the corner next to me—
watching you trace its pages,
like you trace my skin.
I watch you,
listening to the words fall from your lips.

And you pause . . .
brush the hair out of my face,
look into my eyes
and then to my lips;
and you tell me,

him

"In this moment—
in this very moment,
you
look
like
poetry."

her

Your hands can heal.

In the way they run their fingers over my body—
like water cleansing my every sinful thought,
as if they were touching the deepest depths of me.
And suddenly it is telling us our connection before
was nothing but misfire,
a starving spark begging for oxygen to breathe into it.
We were twin flames in separation
just waiting to burn for one another.

Your touch,
is something spiritual.
An awakening,
a revival—
recovery.

her

I am intoxicated by you:
the poison flooding my veins,
running wild in my bloodstream,
burning my lungs,
chemicals reacting,
overriding my system,
driving me absolutely mad,
lovesick—
the best kind of insane.

It's always been you.

epilogue

and
we
were,
effortlessly.

–

*even
after
all
this
time.*

About the Author

Paige Renee Wedman is an endless creator, drawing artistry in all ways. She is a poet, author, silversmith, photographer, model, and whomever else she decides to be in the years to come. She believes there is art and poetry all around us, in every aching form of existence. It is up to us to find it and embrace it, along with ourselves, in every phase of healing and growth—to rise from the brokenness. Sometimes the hidden gems in life are within the heartache. She hopes to inspire others to live and love authentically and bravely, all the while running after their own wild.

Visit

www.prwpoetry.com & **@p.r.w.poetry**

or contact

prwpoetry@gmail.com

for more information.

He is everything:
the poison,
the ruin,
the antidote,
the cure.

He is everything . . .
and *everything,*
          all at once.

But then she remembered,
it was also her;
and so was she.